HABITAT DESTRUCTION

*First published in
the United States in 1991 by*
Gloucester Press
387 Park Avenue South
New York NY 10016

Library of Congress Cataloging-in-Publication Data

Hare, Tony.
    Habitat destruction / Tony Hare.
        p. cm.-- (Save our earth)
    Includes index.
    Summary: Examines factors threatening
various animal and plant habitats, such as
pollution and depletion of our natural resources,
explaining what we can do to conserve and
preserve our planet instead.
    ISBN 0-531-17307-0
    1. Man--Influence on nature--Juvenile
literature. 2. Natural resources--Juvenile
literature. 3. Pollution-- Juvenile literature.
4. Nature conservation--Juvenile literature.
[1. Conservation of natural resources. 2.
Pollution.] I.Title. II. Series: Hare, Tony. Save
our earth.
GF75. H36 1991
333.95'16--dc20   91-8402 CIP AC

Printed in Belgium

The publishers would like to
acknowledge that the
photographs reproduced within
this book have been posed by
models or have been obtained
from photographic agencies.

Design	David West Children's Book Design
Editor	Elise Bradbury
Picture research	Emma Krikler
Illustrator	Ian Moores

The author: Dr. Tony Hare is a
writer, ecologist and TV host. He
works with several
environmental organizations,
including the London Wildlife
Trust, the British Association of
Nature Conservationists, and
Plantlife, of which he is Chairman
of the Board.

The consultants: Mark Cocker is a
freelance writer and naturalist
living in Norwich, Norfolk.

Jacky Karas is a Senior Research
Officer with Friends of the Earth.
Prior to this she was a Senior
Research Associate at the Climatic
Research Unit at the University of
East Anglia, Sussex, England.

SAVE OUR EARTH

HABITAT DESTRUCTION

TONY HARE

GLOUCESTER PRESS

London · New York · Toronto · Sydney

CONTENTS

INTRODUCTION

Worldwide, people are changing the face of the earth. Wild areas are cleared for farming and to build roads and expand cities. Our factories, cars and power plants poison the environment with polluting gases and chemical wastes. Many of the ways that we transform the environment destroy habitats: the "homes" of plants and animals.

Living things have evolved over millions of years to survive in certain environments. When these areas are destroyed, wildlife cannot always adapt to the new conditions and can die out. As a result of human activities, tens of thousands of species of plants and animals face extinction.

People can also suffer from habitat destruction. For example, clearing the forests off the Ethiopian highlands has led to tons of soil being washed away, causing crop failure and starvation for the people. There is the future to consider, too; plants and animals provide essential food and medicine sources. If species are made extinct their potential value will never be known.

The scale of destruction of habitats worldwide is enormous. Swamps, forests, grasslands and jungles are being cleared at an increasing rate. Coral reefs, called the rainforests of the ocean because they are so rich in life, are threatened around the world. We must contain the damage to habitats now so that they remain a valuable resource for the future.

◀ **Part of the Amazon rainforest in Brazil is burned to make room for cattle ranching. The wildlife that thrives here will move on, if it survives the destruction. Half of the world's tropical rainforests have already been cut down. Each year, an area the size of Great Britain is cleared.**

POPULATION EXPLOSION

The world's human population is growing fast. Every day about 230,000 babies are born, adding to the five billion of us who already inhabit the planet. Since you started reading this page, about 25 people have come into the world. Children are important for the future, but growing populations can damage habitats. More and more undeveloped areas have to be cleared to provide people with food, resources and places to live.

One reason for the population explosion is that advances in medicine in the last 200 years have helped people live longer. Yet in poor countries good medical care is not always available and many infants die. Families in these areas rely on having many members to bring in money or to farm the land. And because survival is uncertain, women have more children in case some die. Families get poorer as they struggle to feed all their children. As their poverty grows, they are forced to clear wild habitats in order to farm.

▼◄ The world population in A.D. 10 stood at around 250 million. It is expected to reach six billion by the year 2000. Nearly half of these people now live in cities. The expansion of urban areas has been particularly rapid in poor countries as people move from the countryside into the city to look for work. Often they cannot find jobs and end up in poverty-stricken shanty-towns which grow up around the edges of cities. In this way urban areas spread into wild land.

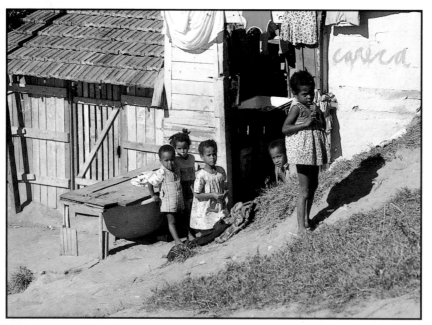

YEAR   AD14   1000   1500

▼ Modern farming produces enough food to feed the world, but if the population keeps growing, soon it may not be able to keep up.

POPULATION IN HUNDREDS OF MILLIONS

40

30

20

10

5

1750   1900   1975   2000

HABITAT DAMAGE

The increase in population leads to a demand for more houses and industries, and the need for food requires more acres of cropland to be cultivated. Finding land for these uses often means the replacement of wild habitats with human-made environments.

Agricultural land covers 9 million square miles of the world's land surface. This area represents nearly all of the land on our planet that is easily cultivated, because ice, mountains and deserts account for a large percentage of the earth's surface. Much of the farmland currently under cultivation is being damaged as farmers try to squeeze more crops out of the soil. This means that the soil may not be fertile in the future, creating the need for new farmland. This is likely to put increasing pressure on the world's remaining wilderness.

Many other types of development demand land. Roads, industry, mines and dams all need land, and their construction often means the disappearance of some habitats and the disruption of others.

Farming can often cause pollution, which damages habitats. Modern agriculture uses fertilizers, which help plants grow, and pesticides, which kill pests. Pesticides can also kill other living things. Fertilizers can wash into water habitats and pollute them.

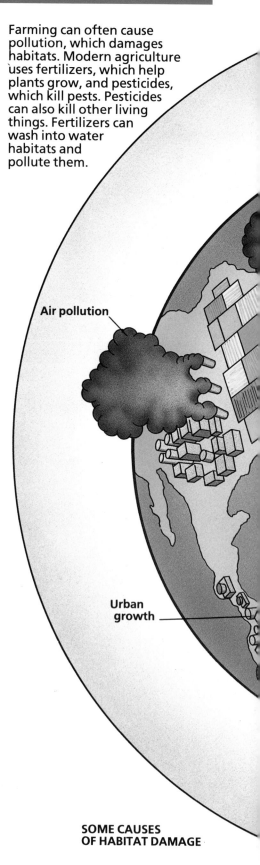

Air pollution

Urban growth

SOME CAUSES OF HABITAT DAMAGE

▲ **Although population growth in the richer countries of the world is low, the people in these countries use far more resources than those in poor countries do. Extracting resources** **damages habitats. The copper taken from this mine in Utah will go to make wire or pipes, but the mountain will never be the same. Vast amounts of rock are destroyed, disrupting the area's wildlife.**

Cities have factories that dump their wastes into the ground and water. Some of these wastes are very poisonous to living things.

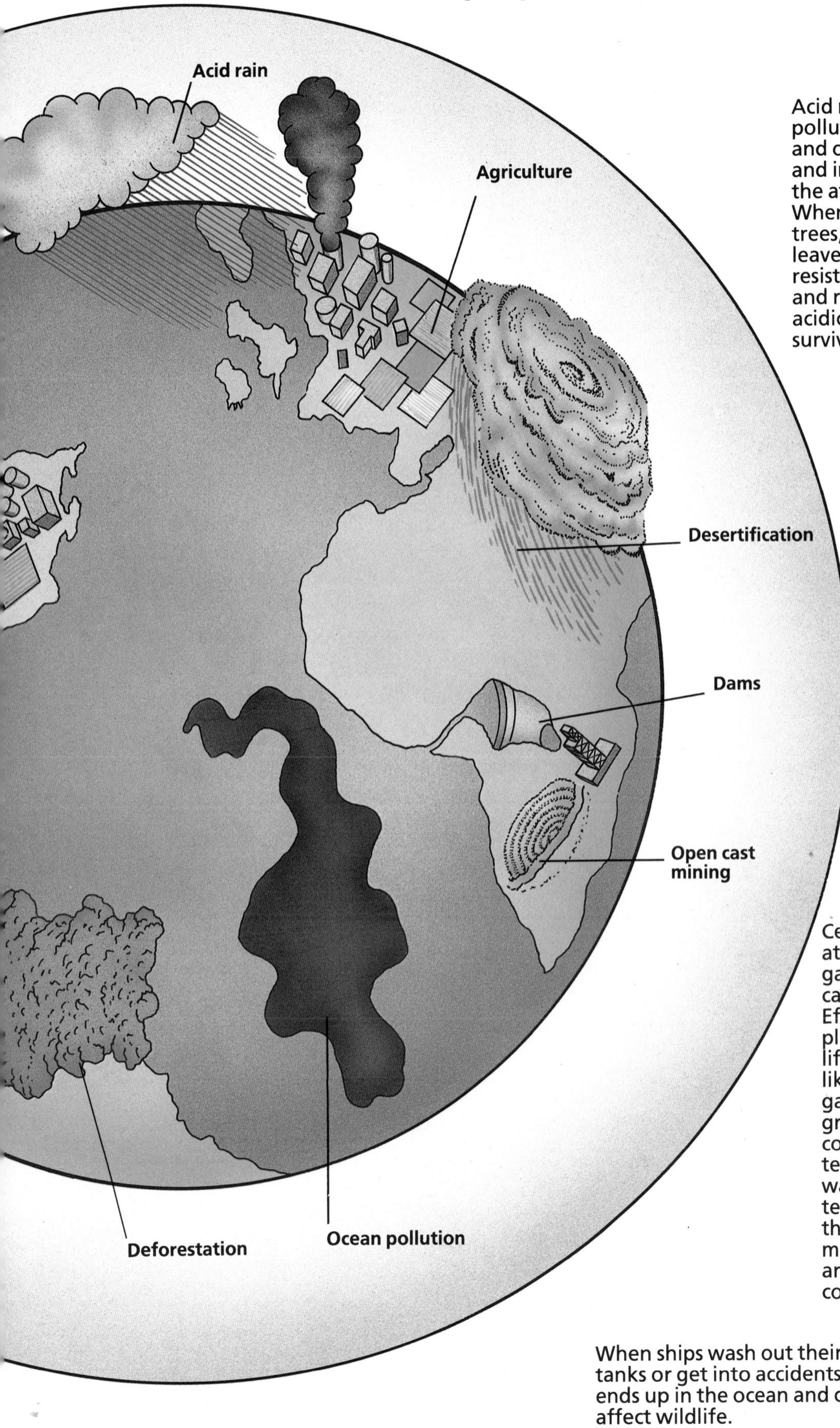

Acid rain

Agriculture

Acid rain is caused when air pollution from burning coal and oil in power stations, cars and industry meets water in the atmosphere, forming acids. When acid rain falls often on trees, they may lose their leaves or become unable to resist pests and diseases. Lakes and rivers can become too acidic for living things to survive.

Desertification

Dams

Open cast mining

Certain gases in the atmosphere (greenhouse gases) trap heat. This is called the Greenhouse Effect and it keeps our planet warm enough for life. But human activities, like burning coal, oil and gas, increase the amount of greenhouse gases. This could raise the earth's temperature, causing global warming. Increased temperatures could disrupt the climate and change many habitats. For instance, areas which are already dry could become deserts.

Deforestation

Ocean pollution

When ships wash out their oil tanks or get into accidents, oil ends up in the ocean and can affect wildlife.

OVEREXPLOITATION

Overexploitation means using a resource until it either runs out or is so damaged that it can no longer be used. This threatens habitats throughout the world. When we overuse habitats it undermines their ability to provide resources into the future.

Grasslands are ideal for wild grazing animals and for raising livestock, like cattle. But if too many animals are grazing, the grass cannot grow quickly enough to keep pace. As the land is stripped of vegetation, the soil becomes exposed and can be blown or washed away. Then no plants can grow back and both wild and domestic animals lose a habitat.

The oceans are also overexploited. They provide us with vital food resources. But in recent years we have been catching more and more fish with equipment like drift nets, which extend for miles. This causes a serious decrease in the numbers of some kinds of fish. All living things in a habitat play an important role, and if species are removed, the whole system can be disrupted.

▼ **Cattle have overgrazed the dry grassland south of the Sahara Desert. Plants help to recycle rainfall by giving off moisture from their leaves. When the vegetation is stripped away, the region becomes drier. Millions of people are affected by drought in this part of Africa, and wild animals like cheetah, gazelles and antelope which used to roam here have lost their habitat.**

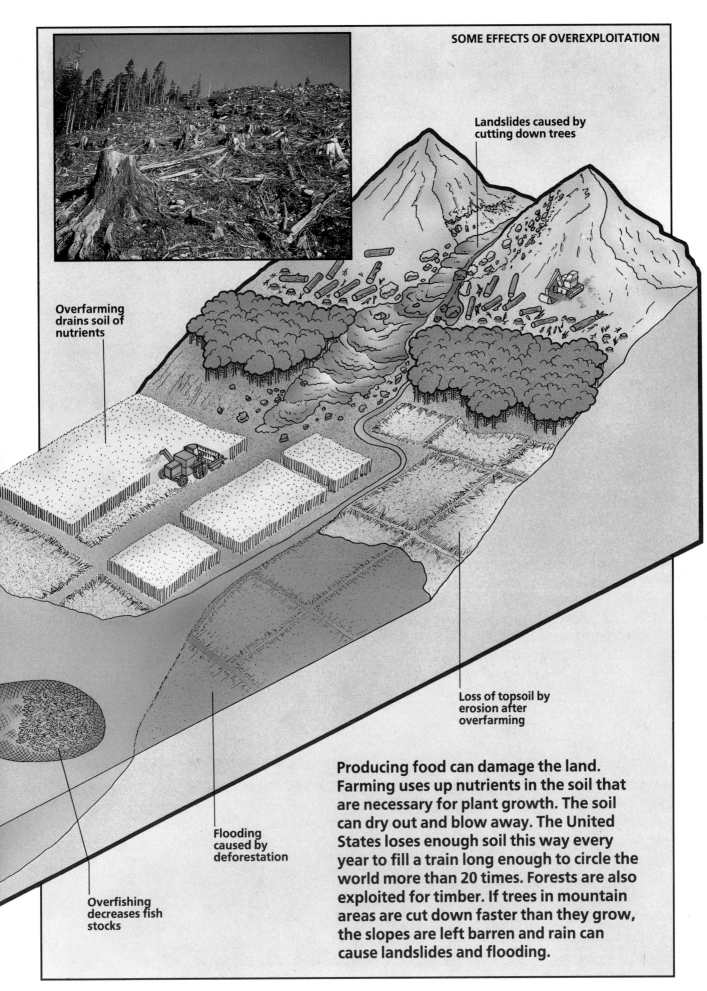

Landslides caused by cutting down trees

Overfarming drains soil of nutrients

Loss of topsoil by erosion after overfarming

Flooding caused by deforestation

Overfishing decreases fish stocks

Producing food can damage the land. Farming uses up nutrients in the soil that are necessary for plant growth. The soil can dry out and blow away. The United States loses enough soil this way every year to fill a train long enough to circle the world more than 20 times. Forests are also exploited for timber. If trees in mountain areas are cut down faster than they grow, the slopes are left barren and rain can cause landslides and flooding.

WETLANDS

Wetlands include saltmarshes and mangroves, which are found on coasts, and freshwater swamps and marshes, which occur along rivers and lakes and where the land regularly floods. Wetlands' mixture of water and land and their range of vegetation – from waterweeds to trees – provide homes for thousands of species. Many rare birds depend on wetlands as feeding and breeding areas. In South American marshes, jaguars stalk their prey through the vegetation.

Wetlands are also valuable to people. Two-thirds of the fish we eat depend on coastal wetlands at some stage in their life. Wetlands prevent flooding by taking up water from rivers, and their weeds can filter water by trapping pollution. For example, Hungary uses its peat bogs to filter waste from sewage plants.

Worldwide, wetlands are under great threat. Burma, Pakistan, Bangladesh and Malaysia have all lost half of their original wetlands. Many have been drained to create farmland. In Africa, planned irrigation programs and other projects like dams will destroy vital wetlands.

▼ One of the major threats to wetlands is that they can be turned into very good farmland when drained. Channels are dug so that water drains from the land. The dry land can then be used to grow crops. This method has been used in Florida's Everglades for 100 years. However, the price is the loss of fish breeding grounds and bird habitats. Some people believe that one way to manage wetlands is to use them in their natural state: for fish farming, for example. If done carefully this could provide food and make money while maintaining a healthy habitat for wildlife.

► The Okavango delta in Botswana is home to many birds, which nest in its marshy grasses. Part of the Okavango is endangered by a plan to reroute the river which feeds the marshes in order to provide water for villages.

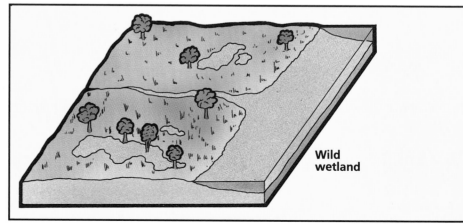

Wild wetland

▼ Skunk cabbage thrives in waterlogged conditions, along with many varieties of reeds. The crocodile is a wetland predator found in tropical regions. Hidden below the water except for its eyes and nostrils, the crocodile will approach its prey unseen. Crocodiles feed mainly on fish.

Ditches are made to drain the water away

Crops can now be planted

FORESTS

The world's forests range from the dark, cold conifer woods that ring the Arctic, to the humid rainforests that form a broken band through the tropics. Forests help to regulate the climate by recycling moisture. They also prevent erosion of the soil as the roots of the trees absorb water and the leaves break the fall of the rain. Forests are the homes of many birds, mammals, insects and plants. The bristlecone pines of the Rocky Mountains are the oldest trees in the world; some were just seedlings 4,500 years ago.

Forests have always provided us with firewood and timber for building. Other resources they supply include fruit and medicines. About a quarter of the world's most important medicines are based on rainforest plants. Yet by the year 2000, most of the rainforests will have been destroyed for timber, farming, mining and ranching. Huge areas of European forests have been poisoned by acid rain. One thousand years ago, forests covered half the world's land surface; today they cover only a fifth.

▼ The woods that once spread over temperate lands (between the polar areas and the tropics) have been much reduced by human activities. Ninety percent of the conifer woods of the northwest United States has been cleared by loggers. Further south, where broad-leaf woods grow in soil which is ideal for farming, only isolated islands of trees remain in a sea of farmland. This has also occurred in many European countries.

▲▶ The squirrel monkey of Latin American rainforests is just one of many species affected by rainforest destruction. In the last 200 years, Africa has lost 52 percent of its rainforests, Asia 42 percent and Latin America 37 percent. The greatest loss has been from shifted cultivation. This is when poor farmers clear patches in the jungle to grow food. The soils are poor and cannot stand farming for long. Then the cultivators have to move on and clear more forest. Saving the forests depends on helping the poor to survive by using the forest's resources without damaging the area.

THREATS TO THE RAINFOREST

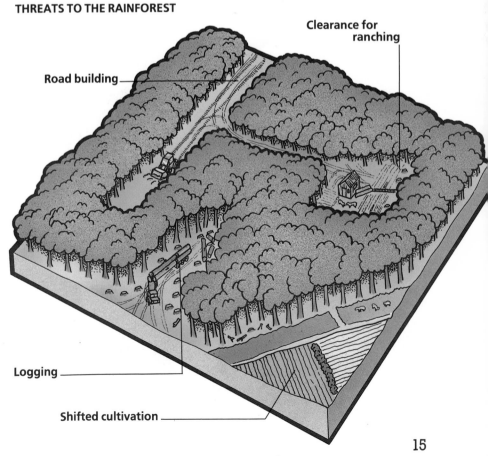

Clearance for ranching

Road building

Logging

Shifted cultivation

GRASSLANDS

The world's grasslands range from the savannas of Africa to the steppes of Asia and the prairies of North America. They are places where dry summers, cold winters, natural fires and heavy grazing stop trees from taking over. The vast African savannas support some of the world's best-known wildlife, such as lions, giraffes, zebra and elephants. Grasslands also support cattle and goats, but if there are large numbers of them, they eat the grass faster than it can grow. With the ground bare, rain and wind carry away the soil which is necessary for plants to grow. The land then turns to desert.

▼ Desertification threatens the livelihoods of a fifth of the people in the world. On the edges of deserts, wind can blow sand over deforested and eroded land. Both China and India have planted tree "walls" to provide a barrier to stop advancing sand dunes. Overgrazing and overfarming are the main causes of desertification.

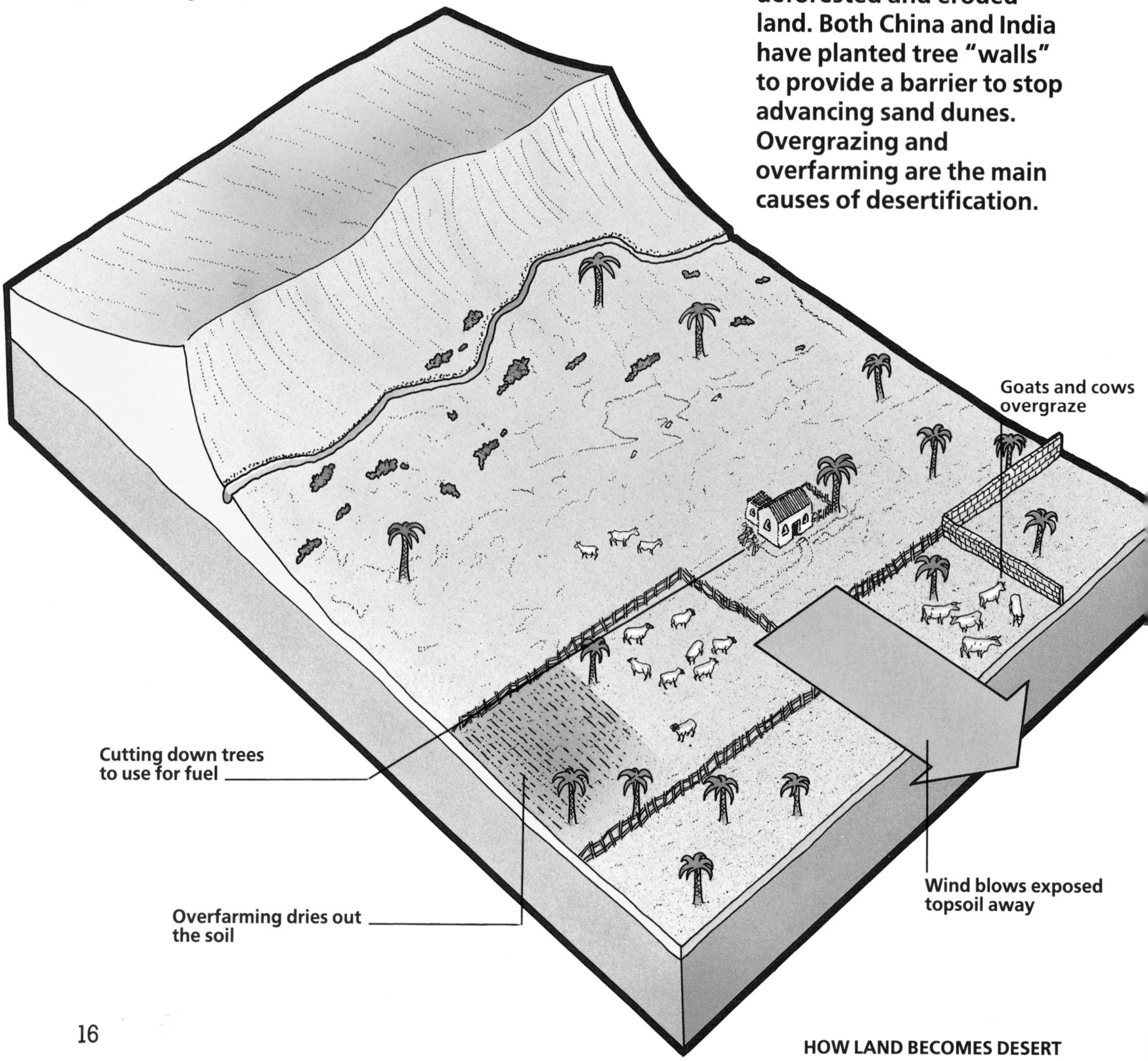

Goats and cows overgraze

Cutting down trees to use for fuel

Wind blows exposed topsoil away

Overfarming dries out the soil

HOW LAND BECOMES DESERT

This process, called desertification, particularly occurs on the edges of deserts and in dry regions. Overgrazing is not the only cause. Grasslands are often converted to farmland, for crops like wheat and cotton. The crops use up all the goodness in the soil, which becomes too dry to support any vegetation at all. In Africa, desertification is made worse as many people rely on firewood for cooking and heating. Trees protect the soil from erosion. When they are cut down, the soil is left exposed to the sun and wind. Up to 30 percent of the world's land surface may be on the verge of becoming desert.

◀▼ Wildlife thrives in a wild grassland like a South American pampas, a North American prairie or a European meadow (above left). Flowers are abundant and they supply insects with food. Grazing animals like deer feed on the plants. But when wild grasslands are replaced by crops, such as fields of wheat, or fast-growing pasture grasses for grazing, such as ryegrass (below), the native wildlife disappears. Pesticides kill off the insects and reduce the food supply of birds and small mammals. Deer are shot if they graze in croplands. Prairie dogs were nearly exterminated by farmers as the North American grasslands were replaced by pastures and farms.

17

FRESH WATERS

Fresh water makes up less than one percent of the water in the world. However, all forms of life depend on water. Human life would be impossible without it. We drink it, use it to water gardens and crops and use it in industry.

Many freshwater habitats have been altered by people. Rivers have been dammed, flooding the land around them which wildlife like beavers depend on. Dams also block the passage of salmon which swim upstream to breed. Some rivers are deepened to allow ships to pass through, disrupting the living things on the riverbed.

Lakes and rivers are also used to dump our wastes. Sewage from cities and chemicals from factories are discharged into waters around the world, poisoning wildlife. The Ganges River in India is dangerously polluted with human and animal sewage. The water from the Vistula River in Poland is so polluted with chemicals that it cannot even be used for industry. Fertilizers washed off farmland are a major pollutant in North American and European fresh waters.

▼ Remote mountain lakes, like this one in Canada, look pure and untouched. But even they can be affected by pollution. Acid rain falls everywhere, and it has a particularly bad effect on freshwater lakes and streams. In southern Norway, four out of five rivers and lakes are too acidic for fish to survive.

▲ Fresh waters are home to many living things. If the water is contaminated with wastes, wildlife can die.

▶ Water held in rocks below the earth's surface is known as groundwater. Half the United States' drinking water is taken from groundwater. The top level of groundwater is known as the water table. Streams often begin where the water table meets the surface of the ground. By drilling a well into the rocks, water can be extracted. But as water is pumped out, the level of the water table falls, leaving the stream habitat dry between the old and the new water tables.

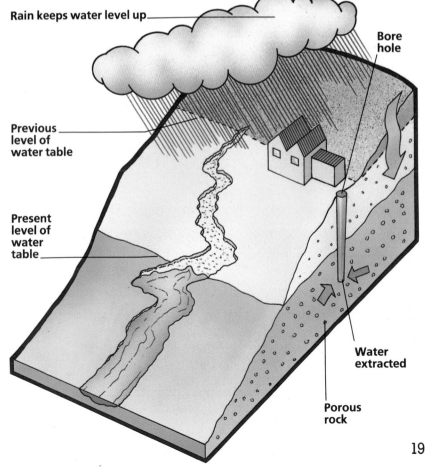

Rain keeps water level up

Bore hole

Previous level of water table

Present level of water table

Water extracted

Porous rock

SEAS AND COASTS

Most of the earth's water is in the seas, which cover about three-quarters of the globe. The sea has long provided us with food. Nearly a quarter of the protein eaten in the world comes from the oceans. Seas also supply other resources, like oil, salt, metals and sand.

However, the immensity of the oceans does not mean they cannot be damaged. If fish are caught faster than they can reproduce, their numbers decline seriously. Scientists believe many major fisheries have been overexploited in recent years. Pollution from oil, sewage, factory wastes and pesticides is also causing problems. Sewage dumping in the Mediterranean has led to huge local growths of algae which cause the oxygen in the water to be used up, suffocating other sea life.

Coasts receive the largest amounts of ocean pollution, so they are the most damaged places in seas. Coastal habitats are also threatened by building projects like tourist developments. Another potential danger to coasts is global warming, which could raise sea levels, flooding low-lying areas like the Nile delta.

▼ ► Mangrove swamps lie along many muddy tropical shores. They provide important habitats for fish. Some 90 percent of fish caught in the Caribbean depend on mangroves at some stage in their life cycle. Many mangrove swamps have been developed for fish farming. The mangrove trees are also cut for timber or to expand farmland and cities. In 1991, a large oil slick released during the Gulf War threatened mangrove habitats in the Persian Gulf. Worldwide, seas and coasts are damaged by wastes which are piped into oceans.

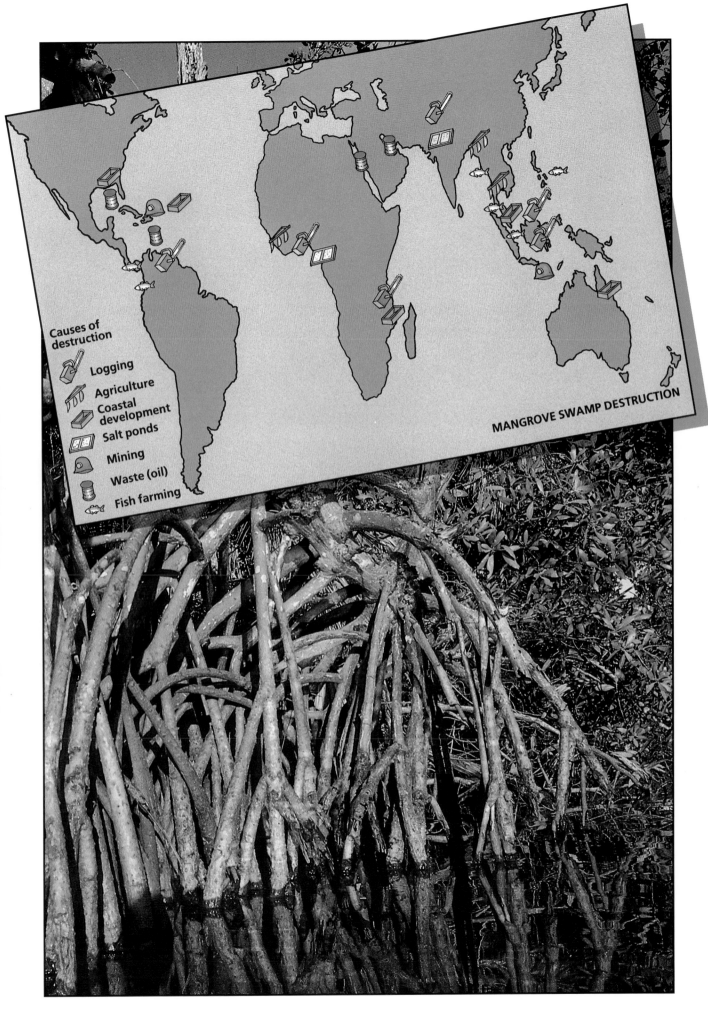

Causes of destruction

Logging

Agriculture

Coastal development

Salt ponds

Mining

Waste (oil)

Fish farming

MANGROVE SWAMP DESTRUCTION

21

MOUNTAINS

The peaks of high mountains are too cold and windy for much to survive. But many well-adapted plants and animals live farther down the mountainsides. Mountain goats and sheep have superb balance, enabling them to reach high ledges. Plants grow close to the ground, which protects them from the drying, chilling wind.

People of mountain regions often shape the slopes into flat terraces to grow crops. Mountains are important to people who live at their bases as well. The forests which cover mountains absorb rainfall and release the water gradually to fill the streams and rivers below. Removing these forests leaves the steep slopes barren, which has disastrous effects. Half of the trees on the Himalayan mountains in Nepal have been cut down, leading to landslides which have buried whole villages. Flooding also occurs during periods of heavy rain. Recently, Nepal has tried to reverse this process by paying villagers to replant trees to stop erosion.

▼ The Alps are Europe's best-known mountains. Ibex (shown below), which once faced extinction, are now protected and roam the mountainsides in larger numbers. However, the forests are suffering from air pollution caused partly by vehicle traffic on roads through the mountains. Added to this is the pressure from tourists. The European countries through which the Alps extend are becoming increasingly concerned to protect them.

CAUSES OF MOUNTAIN HABITAT DESTRUCTION

Global warming
Plants and animals suited to high, cold mountain habitats could find their environment changing if global warming raises temperatures. They may not be able to adapt.

Building
Tourist developments are built in mountain habitats for hikers and other visitors. Switzerland has thousands of hotels covering the equivalent of 15,000 football fields.

Acid rain
Rain and snow carried from industrial areas is acidic. Acid rain damages trees' leaves and can also harm the soil, making it difficult for plants to thrive.

Recreation
Millions of people visit mountains to sightsee and explore on foot or by ski, car or bicycle. These activities can wear away soil and vegetation.

Overgrazing
Meadows and mountain grasslands are ideal for grazing animals, but large numbers of them will strip the area of plants. This could lead to erosion.

Reforestation
Tree planting has been seen as one solution to rapid deforestation. However, forest planting can also lead to habitat loss. Timber plantations are often made up of just one type of tree and provide a very limited environment for wildlife.

23

SAVING HABITATS

Worldwide, concern to protect the environment has been growing. Many people are calling for undisturbed wild places to be made into nature reserves where habitats and wildlife are protected. About three percent of the world's land is now covered by nature reserves.

These reserves have many benefits. They help to safeguard many species from extinction. However, conservation of habitats cannot succeed without the cooperation of the local people. Many countries have recently set up reserves which benefit local communities. New Guinea, for example, has protected its wetlands, but allows local people to continue their traditional way of life as long as they do not do any damage to the reserve. As poverty is one of the main causes of habitat destruction, conservation programs that provide some income for those who live in the area will be most successful. Tackling poverty will reduce the need for people to have many children, thus decreasing another cause of habitat loss: population growth.

▼ **Both wild and human-made habitats can be managed in a sustainable way. This means using the resources they offer without destroying the area. Rainforests are one example. They provide products such as rubber and cocoa pods, which these boys are harvesting without cutting down trees or damaging vegetation. In 1990, Brazil created four reserves for sustainable harvesting in the Amazon rainforest.**

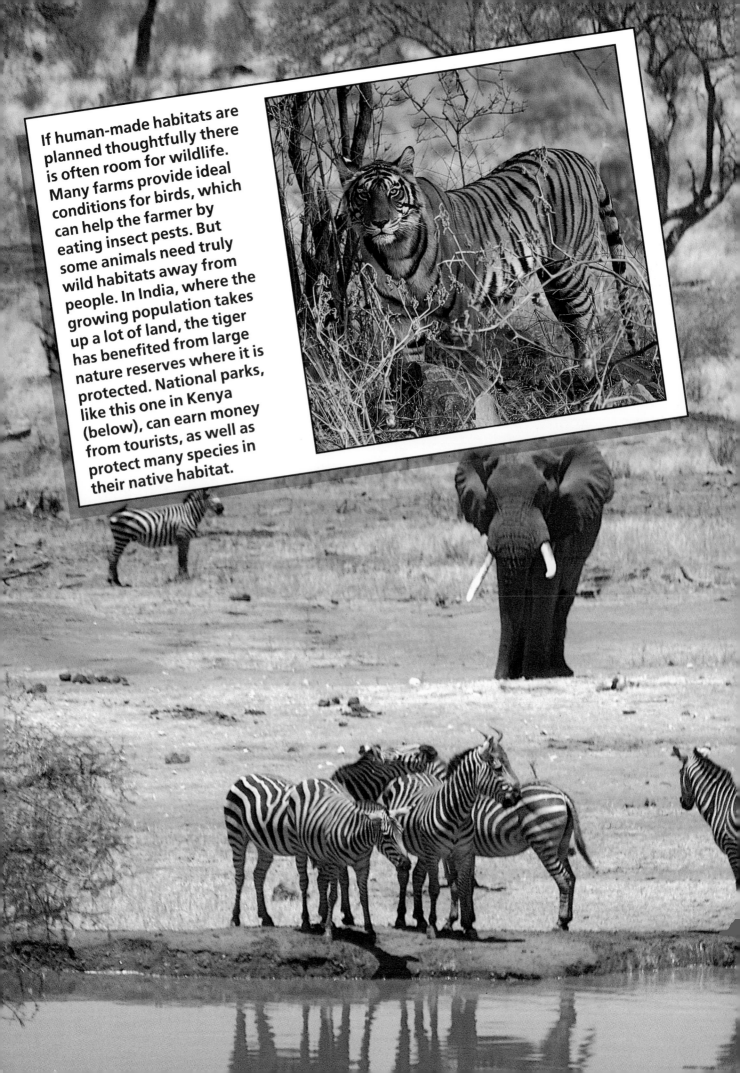

If human-made habitats are planned thoughtfully there is often room for wildlife. Many farms provide ideal conditions for birds, which can help the farmer by eating insect pests. But some animals need truly wild habitats away from people. In India, where the growing population takes up a lot of land, the tiger has benefited from large nature reserves where it is protected. National parks, like this one in Kenya (below), can earn money from tourists, as well as protect many species in their native habitat.

WHAT YOU CAN DO

Habitat destruction is a global problem. However, there are things you can do locally. Perhaps there is an endangered wild area near you which your community is trying to save. Even better, create a wood, a wildflower meadow or a pond by asking a farmer, your local government or your school for some land to be set aside. You can hold a sponsored event with friends to raise money for organizations that try to save habitats or reduce poverty. You can also write to your representative in Congress or the organizations listed below.

Useful addresses:

The Conservation Foundation
1250 24th Street, NW
Washington, DC 20037

Environmental Defense Fund
257 Park Avenue South, Suite 16
New York, NY 10016

Environmental Action Foundation
1525 New Hampshire Avenue, NW
Washington, DC 20036

Greenpeace USA
1436 U Street, NW
Washington, DC 20009

Designing a poster:

One of the most important things you can do is to make more people aware of the problems caused by habitat destruction. One way you can do this is to make a poster to hang up at school.

1) Think up a striking or clever heading for the poster that will grab people's attention.

2) Design an illustration or symbol like the one shown here, or cut pictures out of magazines and make a collage that conveys the main message.

3) Read through this book and try to summarize in about 30 to 40 words what is happening with habitat destruction and why it is important.

4) Again by reading through the book, make some suggestions as to how we can protect vanishing habitats.

5) Include some other information if there is room, such as useful addresses to contact for more information, and suggestions of your own on taking part in creating new habitats for the future.

SAVE OUR HABITATS

BECAUSE OF HUMAN ACTIVITIES, SWAMPS, JUNGLES, FORESTS, GRASSLANDS, DESERTS, LAKES AND THE OCEANS ARE ALL BEING DAMAGED. THOUSANDS OF SPECIES FACE EXTINCTION. IN A FEW DECADES, THERE MAY BE ALMOST NO WILDERNESS LEFT.

WHAT CAN YOU DO?
- EDUCATE OTHERS TO RESPECT THE ENVIRONMENT.
- SET UP YOUR OWN WILDLIFE RESERVE, LIKE A POND OR A SMALL MEADOW.
- GET INVOLVED TO SAVE AN ENDANGERED HABITAT IN YOUR COMMUNITY.

USEFUL ADDRESSES

FACT FILE 1

Habitat neglect

Some habitats are lost through neglect. Europe's lowland heaths are an example of this. Heaths are typically dominated by heather, which covers the land with sheets of beautiful purple flowers in summer. Heath wildlife includes dragonflies, snakes and lizards. Heathlands are also home to some unusual birds, such as the nightjar, which catches insects while flying at night, and the hobby, a small but powerful falcon. Heaths originally came into being when people cleared trees from sandy and gravelly ground in order to graze their livestock. Grazing animals and fires (deliberately started to get rid of old heather and encourage new growth) kept trees from coming back. But during this century, grazing has been abandoned on many heaths. Most sheep now graze on modern human-made pastures. When they are abandoned, heaths are quickly invaded; shrubs and ferns come first, then birch and then oak trees. In the end there is a wood with its own wildlife, but with no place for the specially adapted plants and animals of the heath.

Open heathland

Shrubs, ferns and birch

Oak and birch wood

The debt factor

Over the years, wealthy regions like Europe, Japan and the United States have loaned money to poorer ones. But as these countries, mainly in Africa, Asia and Latin America, fall deeper into debt, they get poorer. In search of money they are forced to further exploit their natural resources, damaging habitats.

Wildlife tourism

If wild habitats bring no income to local people, the residents of the area may be forced to replace them with crops. Wildlife tourism can help the economy and protect habitats. In Rwanda, tourists pay to see mountain gorillas in the wild.

Greening the desert

Desertification is a major problem for millions of people around the world. Planting trees in the desert can help stop erosion and can protect croplands from the wind. This method has been adopted in some dry regions of the Middle East, like on the Arabian peninsula (right). In addition, researchers are attempting to bring rain to deserts. Several North African countries are planning to use artificial trees to generate rainfall. The trees are made of plastic, and during the night they absorb moisture from the air. During the day they slowly release this moisture, cooling the air around them. It is hoped that the cooling effect from the trees will cause moisture from the air to create rain clouds. Libya is planning to plant up to 40,000 plastic trees with the hope of creating a new river in the dry area of the south.

The disappearing seas

The need for water for irrigation, industry and drinking has led to the destruction of many water habitats. The Aral Sea in the Soviet Union has lost at least half of its water since the 1960s. Its area has shrunk by a third. The water has been diverted from the rivers that feed the Aral in order to irrigate cotton and rice crops. As the sea has shrunk, 324,000 acres of wetlands around its edges have dried up, and former fishing communities are now far from the water. The once flourishing fishing industry is dead, and abandoned fishing boats litter the ground. The dry seabed stretches for miles.

FACT FILE 2

Organic farming and gardening

Although farms have replaced many wild areas, they can still be managed in ways that help the environment. Organic farmers use natural methods to protect their crops instead of chemical fertilizers and pesticides. For example, they keep hedges and ponds which provide homes for wildlife like birds and frogs that eat insect pests.

Antarctica

Antarctica is the planet's last great wilderness. It covers 10 percent of the earth's land surface, and together with its waters, it supports a variety of sea life, including penguins, seals, whales and seabirds. It also holds huge reserves of coal and other minerals, which make it vulnerable to exploitation. However, there are increasing calls for it to be protected.

GLOSSARY

Acid rain – rain which is made acidic when pollution from industrial areas and cars reacts with water in the atmosphere. It can damage trees and soil and can acidify lakes. Acid rain is also harmful to health.

Desertification – the process by which dry lands turn to desert. This can be caused by vegetation being grazed away, leaving the soil exposed to rain and wind. Also, excessive farming can remove the fertility from the soil so plants can no longer grow, leaving the ground bare.

Food chain – a network of living things that depend upon each other for food. For example, insects feed on plants and in turn are eaten by birds. Large birds like hawks then feed on smaller ones. If one link in the chain is damaged, for instance by pollution, the whole chain can suffer.

Global warming – gases in the atmosphere, like carbon dioxide, naturally trap heat from the sun-warmed earth. This keeps the planet warm enough for life. But increasing amounts of polluting gases from factories, cars and power plants could trap more and more heat, possibly causing dramatic climate change.

Habitat – any place which is occupied by living things. Habitats include forests, streams, marshes, mountains, gardens, oceans and even brick walls.

Livestock – domestic animals like cattle, pigs and sheep kept by people to provide leather, milk or meat, or to work in the fields.

Nature reserve – an area which is set aside to protect plants and animals. Nature reserves can vary from tiny ponds in school grounds to massive national parks.

Overexploitation – the use of resources at a level which is too high for the supply to continue. One example is overfishing, where fish are taken faster than they can breed. Overexploitation can cause long-term damage to habitats.

Pollution – when substances reach harmful levels in the environment.

Sustainable management – a way of managing the land so that we benefit from it without destroying it. For example, in the Andes Mountains of Peru, local Indians harvest wild plants from the wetlands to provide food, rather than replacing the marshes with farmland.

INDEX

Photographic Credits:
Cover and pages 6, 6-7, 8, 17 bottom right, 20 and 29 top: Zefa; pages 4-5 and 30 top: The Environmental Picture Library; pages 7, 10, 17 top, 18, 22 and 30 bottom: The Robert Harding Picture Library; page 11: Frank Spooner Pictures; page 12-13: Planet Earth Pictures; pages 13 top, 17 bottom left, 25 top and 28: Bruce Coleman; pages 13 bottom, 14, 24 and 29 bottom: Hutchison Library; pages 15, 19 and 25 bottom: Ardea; page 21: Oxford Scientific Films.